TIDAL
STREAMS
EXPLORER
Guide

WILLIAM THOMSON

Imray

William Thomson FRGS is an author, artist and adventurer.

He is founder of *Tide School* and a Fellow of the Royal Geographical Society. William is author and illustrator of *The Book of Tides* and *The World of Tides*, and regularly writes for magazines including Yachting Monthly, Coast, Outdoor Swimmer and Sailing Today.

William lives full-time aboard his yellow catamaran *Luna* with his partner Naomi, their children Ottilie and Arva, and the family's rescued Mallard duck 'Herby'. The crew are currently on a long-term circumnavigation, taking time to fully explore the places they visit while William writes and runs his *Tide School,* teaching people how to 'Seas The Power'.

In addition to sailing, William is a trained PADI Rescue Diver, sea swimmer and surfer. This multi-dimensional approach to adventures brings a practical experience to William's work, which is shared through this series of Explorer Guides - made for anyone who enjoys the sea.

Published by
Imray, Laurie, Norie and Wilson Ltd
Wych House
The Broadway
St Ives
Cambridgeshire
PE27 5BT

+44 (0) 1480 462114
ilnw@imray.com
2021

© William Thomson, 2021

All rights reserved. No part of this publication may be reproduced, transmitted or used in any form by any means, electronic or mechanical, including photocopy, recording or anyinformation storage and retrieval systems, without permission in writing from the Publisher.

British Library Cataloguing in Publication Data.
A catalogue record for this title is available from the British Library.

ISBN 978 178679 294 5

Printed and bound in Croatia by Denona

6	INTRODUCTION	
12	CHANGES WITH **TIME**	
24	CHANGES WITH **PLACE**	
34	**CLUES** FOR EXPLORERS	
50	**PHENOMENA** MADE BY STREAMS	
58	STREAMS DICTIONARY	

We live in a fascinating age of information where accurate forecasts streamed to our phones can tell us exactly what the winds, waves, tides and streams will be doing every hour of the coming days. But what these forecasts do not tell us is how these conditions interact with each other and the coast to create a specific sea state at a certain time and place. The purpose of this series is to fill that gap, equipping you with the skill to take a forecast and use that knowledge to predict what to expect where and when.

Why is this important? Because if you know what is going to happen in an hour around the headland, or tomorrow in the bay, you will be better informed to make decisions that enhance your safety and performance. Those hidden dangers lurking beneath the surface will be less of a threat because you were aware of them long in advance, while precious windows of opportunity will always be made best use of. In short, with these guides at your side you will be one step closer to being in the right place at the right time, safely bypassing the wrong places at the wrong times.

To the untrained eye, the sea can seem like a chaotic environment, puzzling and unpredictable. But with guidance, a natural order appears from the chaos. There is always an explanation for why something is happening, and it is usually a blend of simple factors coinciding - the shape of coastline, time of day, weather conditions, moon phase. In this collection of books we will explore all these factors one at a time, analysing their individual effect on the sea's moods. To achieve this, each guide focuses on a different element (Tides, Streams, The Moon, Winds, Waves, Rips, Clouds, Currents, Stars) and they are organised into two main sections; 'Changes with Time' and 'Changes with Place', with each page analysing the effects of a single variable.

Infographics are an integral role in this work because they are so effective at helping to explain concepts. But when it comes to cycles, such as the moon orbiting the earth or tide waves spinning around oceans, a stationary image can only show one moment in the cycle and you need to visualise the rest. This can be difficult, so to make learning easier there is a collection of DIY models to accompany these guides. The idea is for you to download the designs for free at www.tidalcompass.com using the code EXPLORERGUIDES and assemble the models at home, using them alongside these pages to better understand natural processes.

▶

If you are reading this book you are aware of the sea's power. Although we can train our bodies to be as strong as possible, in a strength contest with the ocean we will lose every time. Even the strongest boats may be overwhelmed by a rogue wave. But luckily we have a secret weapon - the power of our minds. Instead of trying to achieve our objectives with brawn, we can use our brains. These guides will help you to do this by deepening your understanding of nature's forces and sharing ways to harness this energy to your advantage, going further and faster while consuming less of your own precious energy. If our ultimate goal is to be summed up in three words, it must surely be 'Seas The Power'.

William Thomson
Aboard *Luna*, at sea

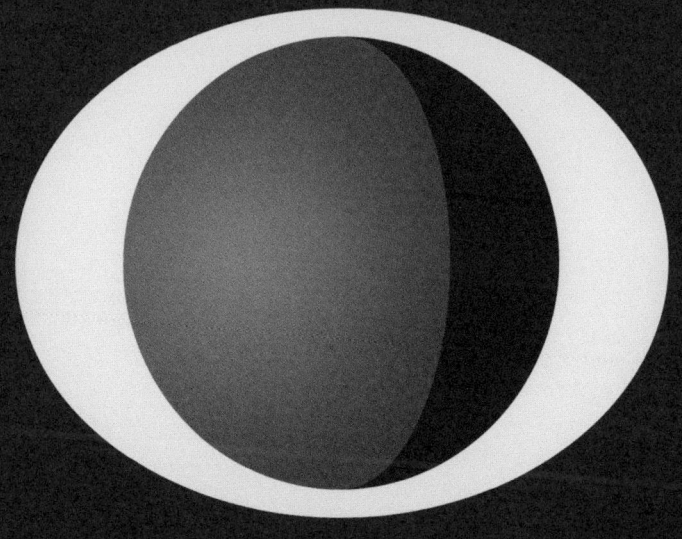

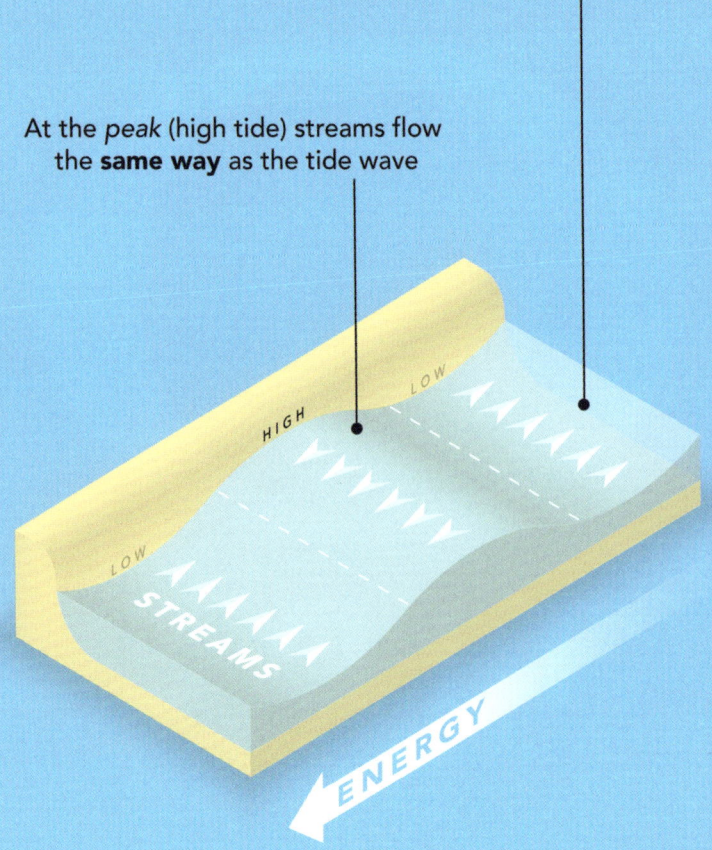

Tidal streams are made by tide waves flowing along the coast

The most important concept to master is that while the peaks and troughs of a tide wave travel in only one direction, the water particles within the wave flow both ways. The best way to understand this relationship is to imagine a tsunami. When a tsunami is approaching land, a clear sign is water draining from the beach; this is because the trough has arrived and although the energy in the wave is travelling towards you, water is being sucked towards the peak, so travels in the opposite direction to the wave. But when the peak arrives, water is pushed along with the wave and it surges up the beach.

Tidal streams are made by this same pushing and pulling effect, but they flow parallel to the shore. These streams determine how far and fast we go, whether the sea is smooth or choppy and what type of dangers we might need to bypass. In short, tidal streams have a profound impact on our safety and performance in tidal waters, so it is important to understand how they work. The purpose of this Explorer Guide is to teach you the key things you need to know and to share ways to 'go with the flow', helping you to explore further and faster with more comfort and safety.

CHANGES WITH
TIME

Tidal streams can change dramatically from one hour to the next and they are constantly speeding up, slowing down and changing direction. Furthermore, what happens one day is different to the next, with the timings and intensity ever so slightly altered.

In this section we will explore the changes in streams that happen when you stay in one place, equipping you with the knowledge to predict what they will be doing at any hour on any day.

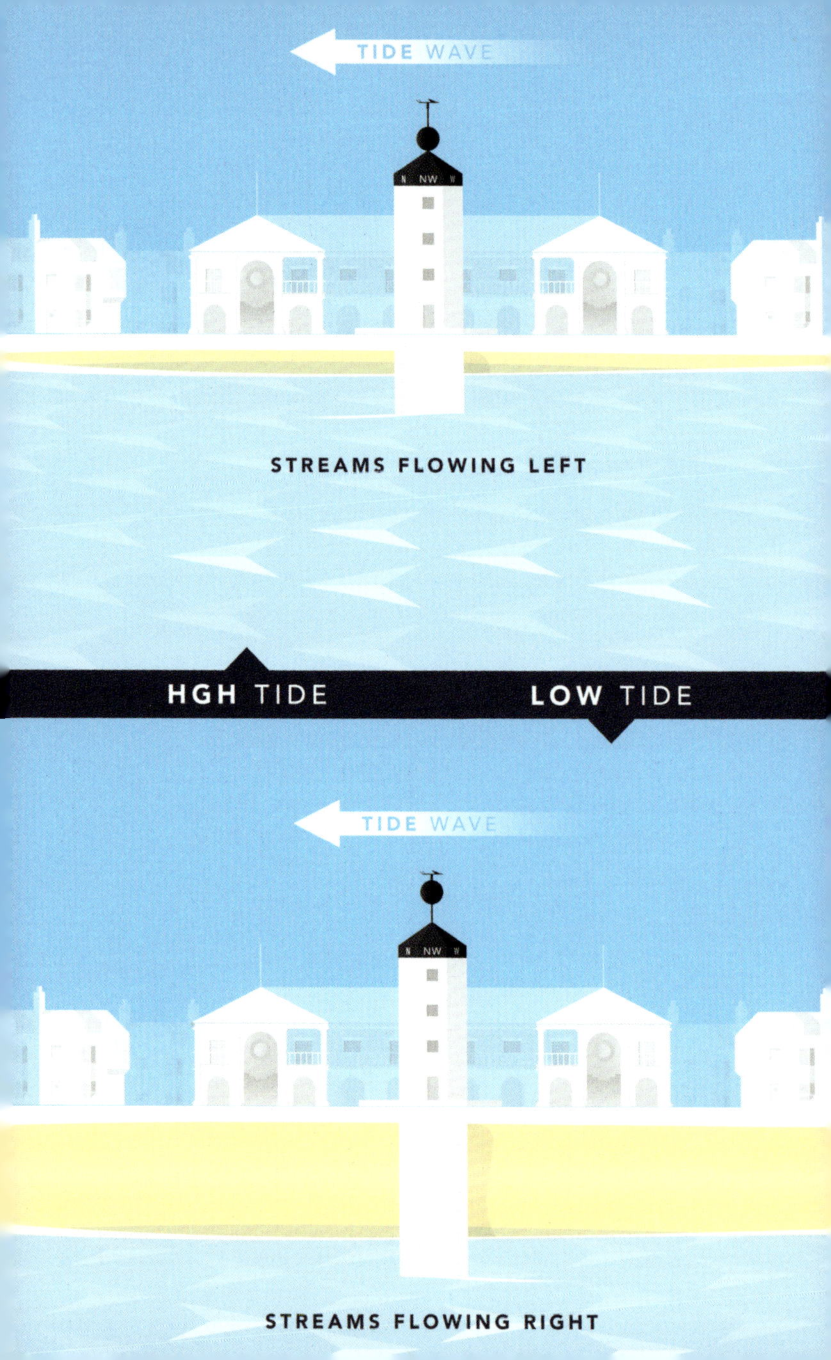
TIDE WAVE
N NW W
STREAMS FLOWING LEFT
HGH TIDE
LOW TIDE
TIDE WAVE
N NW W
STREAMS FLOWING RIGHT

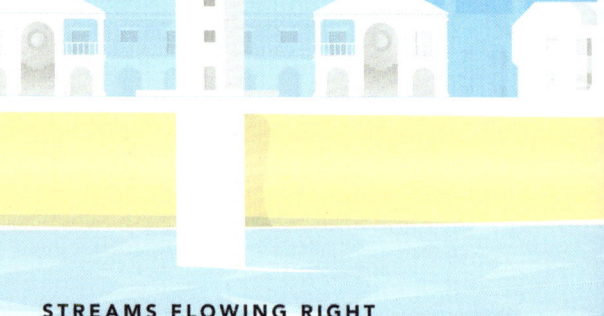

Streams change direction every 6 hours

On an open coast, streams at high tide will almost always be flowing the same way the tide wave is travelling because the peak of the tide wave is literally 'pushing' them along. In contrast, at low tide they flow the opposite way because they are being 'pulled' towards the next peak that is six hours away. In a tidal river or estuary the process is simpler with streams generally flowing inland when the tide is rising and out to sea when the tide is falling (after all, the job of streams is to move water from places with low tide to places with high tide).

This cycle of streams presents exciting opportunities if you want to go fast; going with the flow can dramatically boost your speed without expending any more energy. For example, if your 'speed through water' (STW) is 2 knots and the tidal streams are 2 knots, going with the flow will increase your 'speed over ground' (SOG) to 4 knots; this means that you would travel 4 nautical miles (7.4km) along the coast in just one hour. In contrast, if you were trying to make headway against a 2 knot stream and your STW is 2 knots, your SOG would be 0 knots and you would get nowhere!

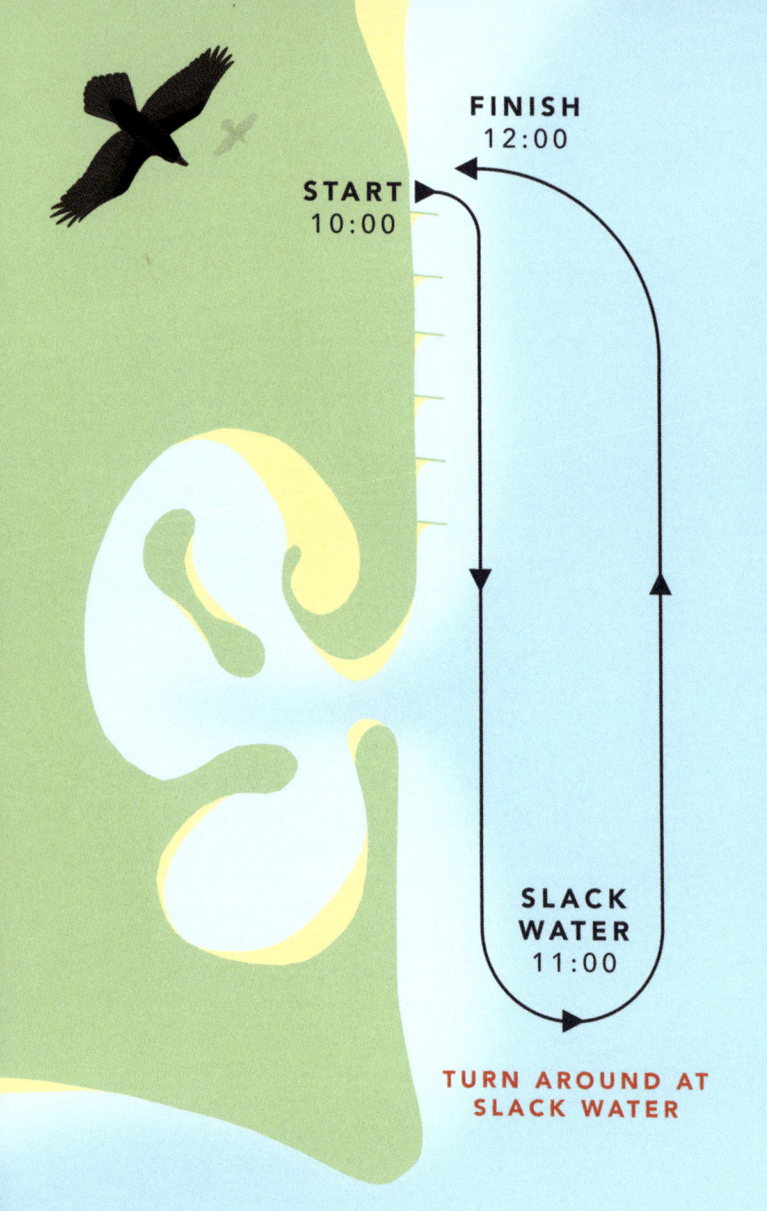

Take note: Streams at harbour entrance will be different, with slack water around high and low tides

Streams change direction at set times before and after high tide

The moment streams change direction is called slack water and this happens at set times before and after high tide. The timing of slack water is unique to each place, but on an open coast it is usually 2 or 3 hours before high tide when streams start flowing in the direction of the tide wave. They then turn around at 3 or 4 hours after high tide and start flowing the opposite way until 2 or 3 hours before the next high tide, repeating the cycle. In rivers and estuaries the pattern is different, with slack water around high and low tides and streams flowing inland as the tide rises then out to sea when the tide falls.

Planning your adventure around the times of slack water allows you to make satisfying return trips along the coast because you can use the streams to take you along the shore and then bring you back to where you started. A simple strategy is to work out how long you want to go out for and plan your departure for half that time before slack water. For example, if you want to go out for two hours, leave an hour before slack water and set off with the stream. After 60 minutes, the currents should turn around and bring you back to where you started.

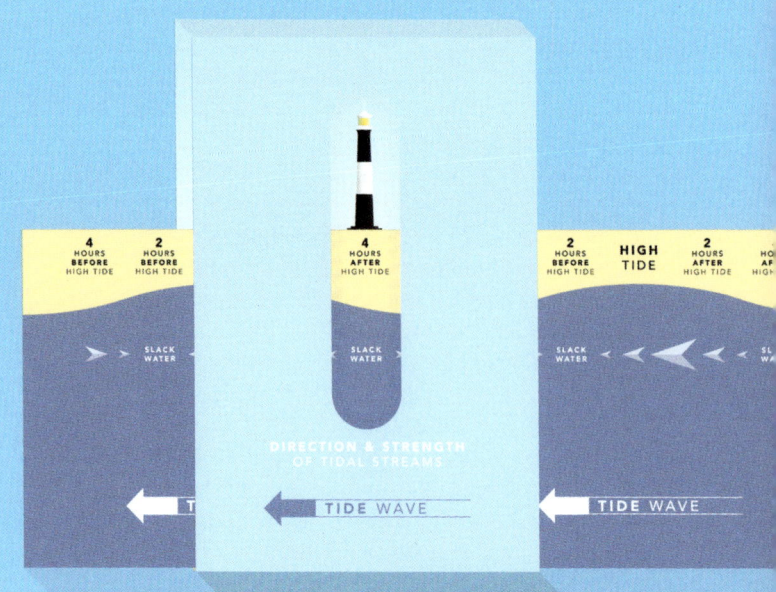

Download and make this model for free
at www.tidalcompass.com

Streams speed up for 3 hours and slow down for 3 hours

Instead of streams simply switching 'on' or 'off' at slack water, they gradually speed up for 3 hours after slack water and then slow down for 3 hours towards the next slack, when they change direction and repeat the cycle the opposite way. This is why sea conditions change hourly and explains why the fastest streams happen three hours either side of slack water. For example, if slack water is at 10am you would expect the fastest streams around 7am and 1pm.

If your activity depends on staying in one place, like diving a wreck or swimming with young children, then timing your trip for slack water will maximise your safety and enjoyment because you do not have to fight against the force of water. In areas with strong streams, this is in fact the only time to safely navigate that place – especially if whirlpools and standing waves develop at maximum flow. However, if you are on an open coast free of these dangers, maximum speed is the perfect time to plan an adventure because it will increase your speed over ground (SOG) and allow you to explore further.

WIND

TIDAL STREAMS

WIND + STREAM = **SMOOTH**

WIND

TIDAL STREAMS

WIND VS. STREAM = **CHOPPY**

Cross-shore winds affect the timing and intensity of streams

When wind and water are blowing and flowing in the same direction the sea will be smooth and the streams are faster - this is because the wind is pushing along the water and enhances the tidal flow. In addition to this, the next slack water will happen later than predicted because when the streams slow down and go slack the surface water is still being pushed by the force of the wind. Once it does turn (sometimes an hour later than expected) streams will be slowed down and the sea will become choppy as the two forces collide.

Kitesurfers and windsurfers often prefer wind vs. tide conditions because you are less likely to get swept along the beach with one of the two forces trying to bring you back. However, if you are swimming, 'wind against tide' can be uncomfortable with the chop splashing into your face when you take a breath. The short seas also make balancing on a paddleboard more difficult, which is why for paddlers and swimmers it is more relaxing to time your trips for when winds and streams are moving together – especially if you organise a one-way trip 'downstream' along the coast.

FULL MOON   NEW MOON

SPRING TIDES

SHORTER PERIODS OF SLACK WATER

FASTER MAXIMUM SPEEDS

FIRST QUARTER   THIRD QUARTER

NEAP TIDES

LONGER PERIODS OF SLACK WATER

SLOWER MAXIMUM SPEEDS

Streams are more intense after the Full Moon and New Moon

When the moon, sun and earth are aligned at the Full Moon and New Moon, their combined gravitational forces make powerful 'spring tides' with higher highs and lower lows (we explain this in *The Moon Explorer Guide*). Because more water is flowing between high and low tide, the tidal streams become more intense and this results in two main consequences. Firstly, slack water becomes shorter; at neaps it often extends to an hour but at springs slack water can last just five minutes. Secondly, the streams flow much faster at springs, sometimes reaching maximum speeds twice as fast as neaps.

This weekly change in intensity has a huge effect on which days are best for particular activities and locations. In some places the streams at springs make it too dangerous (even around slack water) to safely navigate, so you must wait until neaps just after the First Quarter and Third Quarter moon phases when only half the face is visible. However, if the coast is clear of hazards then spring tides provide a fantastic time to 'Seas The Power' and maximise your explorations, both through speeds achieved and distances covered.

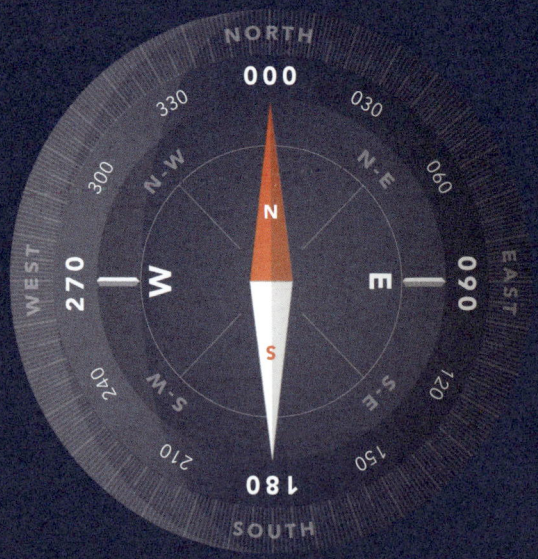

CHANGES WITH

PLACE

When you travel between places you will notice that streams are very different. The times of slack water change, the directions they flow at high tide may be opposite, and the speed water flows can vary considerably.

In this section we will explore the two main factors that make streams change from place to place; topography (shape of the coastline) and bathymetry (shape of the seabed).

Streams are faster at headlands

A headland accelerates water down its side and intensifies the flow at its tip, resulting in tidal streams that are considerably faster than the surrounding waters. When these rapidly flowing streams pass the exposed headland the geography of the coast determines what happens next; the most common scenarios are that they collide with an underwater extension of the land to make a dangerous sea with steep breaking waves called overfalls. But this is not always the case and in some places all that is required for overfalls to form is the wind or swell opposing the tidal streams.

Because of these hazards it is advised to give a wide berth to places with the name cape, bill, point, foreland or ness - sometimes by passing several miles offshore. However, some headlands have a narrow 'inshore passage' (50-100 metres wide) that provides a calm route between the land and the overfalls. This short-cut should only ever be attempted at slack water and never when there is an onshore wind or swell because these can turn the calm zone into a cauldron of breaking waves with no safe way out.

Streams flow the opposite way near obstructions

When streams flow into an obstruction they are accelerated around the side, leaving a 'gap' immediately downstream. To maintain equilibrium, nature ingeniously generates a counter-current flowing the opposite way to the main stream with the job of filling this gap. This is commonly known as an eddy and it comes in all sizes; it could be a metre wide next to a rock or a kilometre in diameter beside an island. What all eddies have in common is that there is very little movement of water in the middle, but the edge is turbulent where the counter-current collides with the main stream and this sometimes generates whirlpools.

If you are travelling against the main stream, finding an eddy can literally 'turn the tide' and give you a boost in the direction you want to go – especially at maximum speed when the streams are fastest and the eddy is stronger. In contrast, if you have planned to go with the flow but find yourself struggling to make headway against the stream, observe your surroundings and look out for any prominent obstructions that may have put you in an eddy. These can be natural like a headland or steep bend in the coast, or a man-made structure like a harbour wall.

Streams are slower in shallower water

In coastal waters, tidal streams flow in the same direction from the surface all the way down to the seabed. However, in deeper water the streams are generally faster than the shallow water closer to shore; local fishermen often use this to their advantage by hugging the shore when they are going into the stream and heading further out when they are going with the flow. This allows them to move around faster while spending less money on fuel and it also provides a useful clue to spot which way the water is flowing.

The changing speed of streams with depth is most noticeable where there is a steeply sloping seabed. For swimmers, kayakers and paddle boarders who can get close to shore without the risk of running aground, if you are heading against the stream it will be considerably easier just a couple of metres from the beach compared to 20 metres offshore. While it is not practical for deep-keeled sailing boats to get quite so close to the beach, there are still gains to be made by finding weaker flows in shallower water if you are travelling against the stream. But if you are going with the flow, heading further out will give you a bigger push in the right direction.

THE CLOSER YOU GET TO THE ENTRANCE
THE FASTER THE TIDAL STREAMS BECOME

WEAKER STREAMS

STRONGER STREAMS

Streams are faster in narrow channels

When water is forced through narrows the streams speed up. This can happen in a passage between the land and an offshore island, a funnel-shaped estuary, a channel connecting two bodies of water or a harbour entrance. Within a man-made harbour, you might find faster streams between structures and in a natural harbour there will be channels of accelerated currents in deeper gaps between sandbars or islands. In short, if you see a narrowing then expect streams to get faster the closer you get to the choke point, with maximum speeds at the narrowest part.

Streams in narrow channels can be powerful even in places where the vertical tide is small; this is most common in natural harbours and lagoons where water from a large basin is concentrated into a single choke point. You must be vigilant here when the wind is onshore (blowing onto the shore) on the ebb (when the tide is falling) because the water and wind are concentrated into the choke point at the entrance and collide with each other to create treacherous seas called 'Overfalls' (see *Phenomena*). Streams flowing out of natural harbours are usually strongest 3 hours after High Tide, so this is when the overfalls will be most intense during an onshore wind.

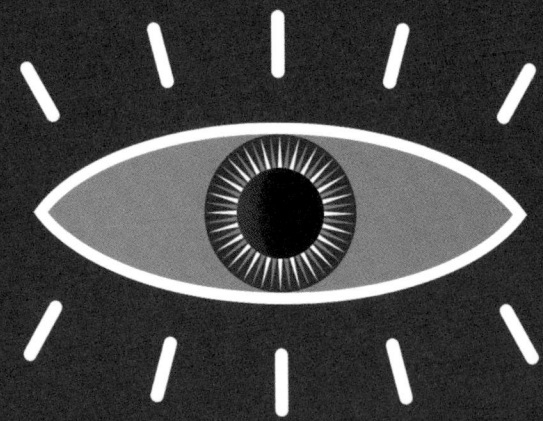

CLUES
FOR THE EXPLORER

Even on days when the sea looks motionless, streams can be racing along the coast. While knowing the time of slack water helps you predict what to expect, it is an invaluable skill to be able to quickly spot the stream when you are out on the water.

In this section we will explore the things to look out for, from boats at anchor to objects in the water, that will help you work out the direction and speed streams are flowing.

STREAMS
ARE FLOWING
LEFT TO RIGHT

BOW WAVE
UPSTREAM

TURBULENCE
DOWNSTREAM

Look out for stationary objects

When streams hit a stationary object like a rock, buoy, post or pier leg it makes an unmistakeable pattern that shows you which way the water is flowing. Here's what to look for:

Immediately downstream of the obstruction you will see a line of disturbed water on either side. This is the 'eddyline' made by counter-currents flowing around the structure; the bigger it is, the faster the water is flowing. Whitewater is a clear sign of powerful streams and is essentially a series of tiny whirlpools; as the streams speed up and the obstructions scale up these can grow into large vortices capable of capsizing a boat and holding down a swimmer, so beware.

A subtler clue is a 'bow wave' on the upstream side of the obstruction. This is where the water hitting the front of the structure bounces back and wraps around the side, making what looks like a set of semi-circular waves. This effect is most pronounced on windless days around man-made objects with symmetrical outlines like posts or buoys, which give another clue by tilting to the side when the streams push against them.

- **C** HW 10:30
- **D** HW 11:00
- **B** HW 09:30
- **E** HW 12:00
- **A** HW 08:30

THE WHITE ARROWS INDICATE
THE DIRECTION YOU WOULD EXPECT STREAMS
TO FLOW AT HIGH TIDE FOR EACH PLACE

Check the time of high tide

It is often easier to find the time of high tide than the time of slack water, so here are some tips for predicting the streams simply by knowing the tide times:

If you are on an open coast, it is highly likely that at high tide the streams will be flowing the same direction the tide wave is travelling. To find this out, simply look at a map and remember that tide waves travel anti-clockwise around a sea in the northern hemisphere and clockwise in the southern hemisphere. In contrast, if it is low tide and you know the direction the tide waves travel, expect streams to be flowing the opposite way (learn why in the *Tides Explorer Guide*).

It is worth noting that there are exceptions to the direction tide waves travel. For example, in New Zealand the tide wave travels anti-clockwise around the islands. To avoid confusion and double check, simply check the tide times for two places on the same stretch of coast; the one that gets high tide last is the direction the tide wave is travelling, so this is the direction streams will flow at high tide (unless it is a river, where streams flow inland as the tide rises and out to sea when the tide is falling).

STREAMS ◄ ◄ STREAMS ►

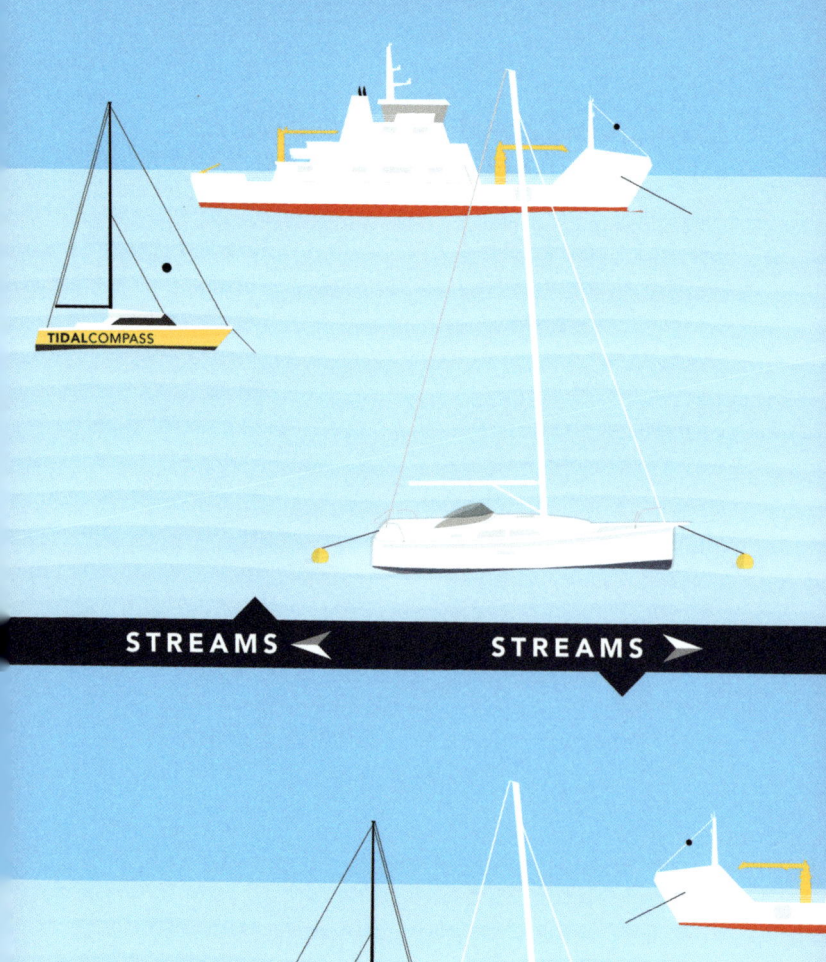

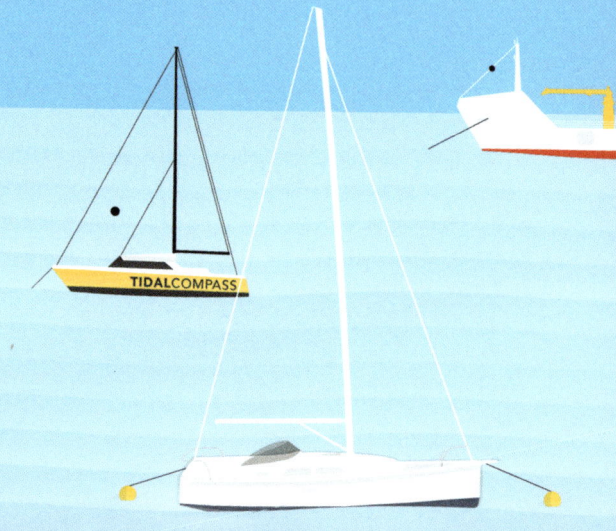

Pay attention to boats at anchor

Boats at anchor should display a single black ball and will have a rope descending into the water from the bow (front). Because a boat at anchor (or tied to a mooring buoy) is connected to a single point, it is free to pivot around in a 360-degree arc. But it does not do this at random; streams flowing into the boat push it away from the anchor or buoy and run evenly down each side so the boat faces upstream. However, there are two variables to look out for; firstly, if the wind is stronger than the stream the boat will face towards the wind. Secondly, make sure the boat is free to swing with the stream; in narrow waterways boats like the white and blue yacht are often secured at the front and back so they will not swing.

For the boats that can move in a full circle, watching them pivot around on a windless day is a clear indicator that the streams are changing direction, so it must be slack water. If this happens to a single boat it may be an anomaly, but if the anchorage is busy and several boats swing around at the same time you can be confident the 'tide has turned'. If you are on a return trip, this is the ideal time to turn around with the streams taking you back to where you started.

2 m

10 metres in 20 seconds = **1 knot**

Observe objects in the water

The sea is full of flotsam and jetsam that can show us the direction and speed streams are flowing. The best guide is something with a small surface area above the water (like a heavy piece of driftwood) because it is less likely to be affected by the wind and you can be confident the water is pushing it along. To calculate the speed of flow, simply time how long it takes to travel a set distance. For example, a floating stick that takes 20 seconds to drift 10 metres will be travelling at around 1.8km/h, which is just under a knot. If you were sitting on a kayak this would take you 1 nautical mile (almost 2km) along the coast in just one hour, without even having to paddle.

You can also use sea foam or bubbles made by waves breaking (this works well with spotting rip currents). It is worth bearing in mind however that when the foam first forms it is more aerated and susceptible to being blown along the surface by the wind. However, as it settles into a thin layer of white bubbles on the surface of a blue sea, you can clearly watch the progress of a single bubble to spot the direction of flow.

STATIONARY BOAT
'SPEED THROUGH WATER'
IS SAME SPEED AS TIDAL STREAMS

Watch what people are doing

People watching has an added advantage over observing objects in the water because you can study their behaviour, especially when they make mistakes, such as when beginners do not taking into account the power of tidal streams. You might see someone on a paddleboard and racing along the shore without paddling. There may be no wind and the sea looks still, but in 20 minutes they can be 1km down the beach (indicating a 1.5-knot tidal stream). When they try to turn back, they cannot make any headway into the stream and end up with a long walk back along the beach. Observing a scene such as this is a clear sign of what the tidal streams are doing.

In narrow channels where currents are accelerated, observing boats making progress against the stream can be useful. The secret is to look around the back of the boat, with whitewater indicating how fast the propeller is spinning. If there is lots of bubbling but the boat is barely moving forwards, it is a clear sign they are trying to make headway into the stream. A similar technique can be used with swimmers and paddlers; if it looks like they are working hard without getting anywhere, they are likely heading into the stream.

SMOOTH
(WIND WITH STREAM)

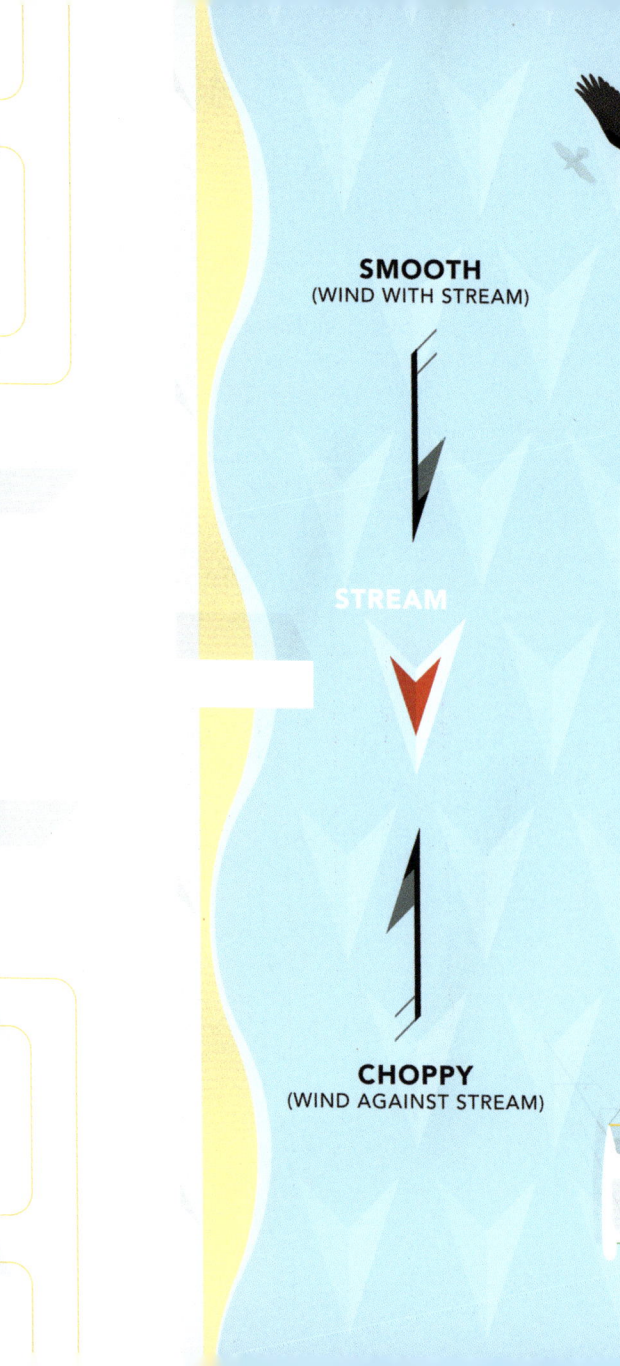

STREAM

CHOPPY
(WIND AGAINST STREAM)

Take note of the wind direction

Earlier in this Explorer Guide we learnt how wind and stream travelling into each other create choppy seas; with this knowledge you can spot the stream by observing the smoothness of the surface.

If there is a strong cross-shore wind in an area known for strong steams and the sea is smooth, this is a clear sign the water is moving the same way as the wind. You can be especially sure of this if the wind stays consistent but the water quickly becomes choppy, indicating that streams have just changed direction and the two forces are now colliding.

In places where winds and streams are funnelled into choke points, 'wind vs. stream' conditions can develop from choppy seas to dangerous overfalls (see *Phenomena*) that should be avoided at all costs. One such place where this famously happens is the 'Alderney Race' between the coast of France and the Channel Island of Alderney, which becomes dangerous even for large boats when the wind is blowing into the tidal stream.

WHEN HALF THE MOON IS ILLUMINATED
HIGH TIDE IS 6 HOURS AFTER FULL MOON TIME

Know the moon phase

Because the timings of streams are connected to high tide, which in turn is synchronised with the moon, you can work out what the tidal streams are doing simply by observing the moon phase. All you need to do is remember the time of high tide at the Full Moon, adding 50 minutes a day. For example, if it is high tide at midday on the Full Moon, streams will be flowing the same way as the tide wave around lunchtime. But a week later at the Third Quarter, when the left half of the moon is visible, high tide will be six hours later so it will be low tide around midday and the streams will take you the opposite direction at lunchtime.

Having an awareness of this connection helps to better understand why the sea behaves the way it does. Because the moon is the leading force that governs the tides and streams, it pays dividends to be aware of its phase each day. Just one benefit of this is that it provides a safety net for human error; for example, if you were to misread the tide times you are less likely to act on that mistake because a voice in the back of your head will be saying the tides do not happen at that time of day at that moon phase. We explain more about this in *The Moon Explorer Guide*.

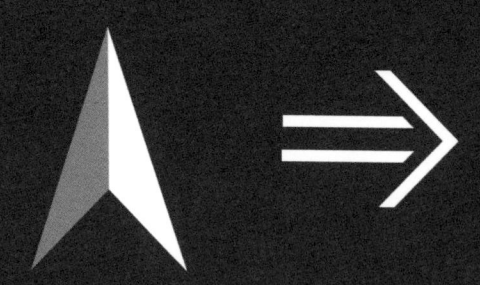

PHENOMENA
MADE BY STREAMS

In places where streams are accelerated (mostly headlands and narrow channels) the fast flowing waters provide a vital ingredient in the creation of dangerous phenomena including whirlpools, standing waves and overfalls.

In this section we will explore what makes these phenomena so you can anticipate exactly where and when they will form, helping you know when to stay away.

WHIRLPOOLS

EDDY

SHAG ROCK

FIN ISLAND

SHAG ROCK

FORELAND

Tidal Streams make Whirlpools

Whirlpools form where opposing streams meet along an eddyline downstream of an obstruction like a rock or island *(see page 28)*. Contrary to popular belief, there is rarely a single whirlpool that stays in one place; instead there are a series of vortices that move along the eddyline, fizzling out where the eddy dissipates downstream of an obstruction. When observing whirlpools you will actually see the two streams collide and wrap around each other, creating a funnel-shaped vortex that descends beneath the surface with spiralling bubbles twisting down into the depths below.

This downward current is strong enough to pull a swimmer to the seabed and whirlpools have been known to suck scuba divers 100 metres under the surface, even with fully inflated buoyancy aids. The powerful opposing currents along eddylines are also a hazard to boats because they can twist a vessel so violently that it capsizes. Luckily, they are easy to avoid because it is easy to predict where and when they will form – downstream of an obstruction in the water when streams are flowing at speed. Simply stay away from those places at those times.

STANDING WAVE

Tidal Streams make Standing Waves

Standing waves are exactly what the name suggests; they are waves that stay in one place. The effect is mesmerising to watch as glassy water flows through the sculpted wave, the only sign of movement being the boiling mass of whitewater downstream. The cause of this phenomenon is usually an underwater ramp close to the surface; the theory goes that water flows down the ramp and creates a wave at the bottom, facing into the stream. This is significant because standing waves usually only form when the streams are flowing one way, which is down the ramp (but the area can still be turbulent when streams are flowing the other way).

For surfers and kayakers, standing waves provide a dream playground because they hang around for hours at a time, compared to beach waves that only give rides measured in seconds. However, for most people the wave and whitewater combination presents a danger to be avoided. There are two main ways to do this. Firstly, pass through at slack water when there is no stream, so no wave. Secondly, if there is a deep channel nearby then navigate through there because the standing waves will only form in the shallows near the underwater ramp.

OVERFALLS CAN EXTEND
SEVERAL MILES OFFSHORE

INSHORE PASSAGE

OVERFALLS ALWAYS FACE INTO THE STREAM
FASTER STREAMS = BIGGER OVERFALLS

Tidal Streams make Overfalls

Overfalls are similar to standing waves but are more chaotic and dangerous. While standing waves create clean faces that can be enjoyed by surfers, overfalls should be avoided at all costs, with steep waves and deep troughs that resemble a boiling cauldron being shaken around. In some places all it takes is a fast stream colliding with the wind or swell to create this lethal phenomenon, but they are most frequently found off headlands where fast currents collide with an underwater reef. While many overfalls can extend for several miles offshore, some headlands have a narrow 'inshore passage' that can be used to slip through in the right conditions (see page 26).

Overfalls are common in harbour entrances all around the world when there is an onshore wind blowing at the same time as the ebb tide. This is because the streams will be flowing out to sea, accelerated by the narrow entrance and then colliding with the opposing wind and swell in the choke point of the channel to create dangerous overfalls. With this in mind, it is unwise to attempt entry or exit through a narrow or shallow harbour entrance in these conditions and it is advisable to wait for slack water or the wind and swell to calm down, whichever comes first.

A
B
C

STREAMS DICTIONARY

Apogean Neap Tide
A neap tide that happens when the moon is at apogee, resulting in weaker tidal streams (see *The Moon Explorer Guide*)

Bar
A ridge of shallow water extending across a river mouth or harbour entrance that is likely to create overfalls

Convergence
A line where two different currents or bodies of water meet, often forming an eddy or whirlpool

Ebb Stream
The direction of tidal streams when the tide is falling

Eddy
A circular movement of water generally found downstream of obstructions

Eddyline
The edge of an eddy, indicated by turbulent water where the counter-current from the eddy collides with the main stream

Flood Stream
The direction of tidal streams when the tide is rising

Gat
A deep channel between two shoals or banks through which streams will flow fast

Lagoon
An enclosed body of salt or brackish water separated from the sea by a reef or low bank. Expect strong streams at the entrance

Lipper
A slight roughness to the sea's surface. This may signify wind against stream conditions

Low Water
The formal way to describe a day's low tide. At this time you would expect tidal streams to be flowing the opposite way to the tide wave

Mole
A massive structure of masonry or large stones extending out to sea; expect an eddy on the downstream side

Knot
A measurement of speed at sea. 1 knot = 1 nautical mile per hour = 1.85kmh

Neaps
A period of weak streams that happen 36 hours after the First Quarter and Third Quarter moon phases

Outflow
The flow of water from a river or estuary out to sea; this will generally happen when the tide is falling

Overfalls
Steep breaking waves caused by fast currents colliding with an underwater obstruction and/or opposing wind and swell

Rate
The speed of tidal streams

Sandwave
A large wavelike seabed found in shallow waters, made of sand and potentially creating overfalls

Set
The direction towards which streams flow

Slack Water
The period of time before and after high tide when tidal streams change direction

Speed Over Ground
Your speed, taking into account the currents (if your speed through water is 4 knots and the current is 2 knots in the same direction, your speed over ground is 6 knots)

Speed Through Water
Your speed, not taking into account the set and rate of currents

Springs
Strong fortnightly tides that happen 36 hours after New Moon and Full Moon, resulting in short periods of slack water and fast tidal streams

Standing Wave
A wave that stays in one place, usually made by a current flowing down an underwater ramp

Tidal Diamond
A position on a chart showing the set (direction) and rate (speed) of tidal streams every hour before and after high tide

Tidal Streams
Currents flowing back and forth along a shore, generally changing direction every 6 hours at slack water

Tide Gate
An area of sea through which tidal streams run with great speed, requiring careful planning to pass through at the optimum time of the tide

Tide Wave
A wave that travels around an ocean or sea (anti-clockwise in the northern hemisphere) bringing high water at the peaks and low water at the troughs

Tideway
A channel through which tidal streams flow

Whirlpool
Water in a rapid rotary motion, commonly found along eddylines

64

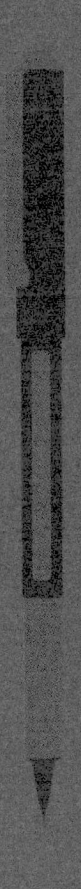

ADVENTURE
PLANNER

If you run out of pages or don't want to write in this book, you can download the adventure planner template and print them yourself at
www.tidalcompass.com

Date ....

Location ....

High Tide __:__ (__.__m) & __:__ (__.__m)

Low Tide __:__ (__.__m) & __:__ (__.__m)

Slack Water __:__ & __:__ & __:__

Streams flow ____ from __:__ to __:__

Streams flow ____ from __:__ to __:__

WIND

__:__   __:__   __:__   __:__   __:__

(N)   (N)   (N)   (N)   (N)

— —   — —   — —   — —   — —
(__)   (__)   (__)   (__)   (__)

NOTES

Date ....

Location ....

High Tide __:__ (__.__m) & __:__ (__.__m)

Low Tide __:__ (__.__m) & __:__ (__.__m)

Slack Water __:__ & __:__ & __:__

Streams flow ____ from __:__ to __:__

Streams flow ____ from __:__ to __:__

WIND

__:__   __:__   __:__   __:__   __:__

(N)   (N)   (N)   (N)   (N)

--   --   --   --   --
(__) (__) (__) (__) (__)

NOTES

Date ....

Location ....

High Tide __:__ (__.__m) & __:__ (__.__m)

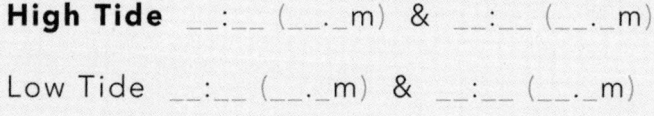

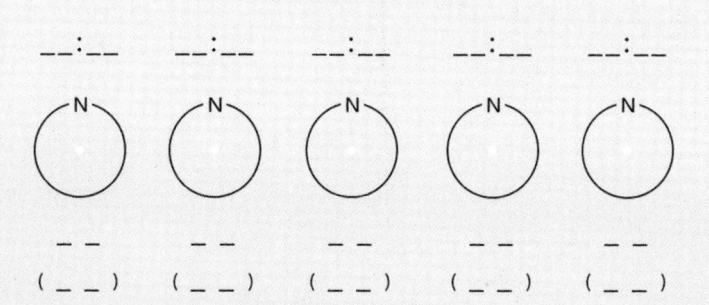

Low Tide __:__ (__.__m) & __:__ (__.__m)

Slack Water __:__ & __:__ & __:__

Streams flow ____ from __:__ to __:__

Streams flow ____ from __:__ to __:__

WIND

__:__   __:__   __:__   __:__   __:__

(N)   (N)   (N)   (N)   (N)

\-\-   \-\-   \-\-   \-\-   \-\-
(__)   (__)   (__)   (__)   (__)

NOTES

More books in the series...

1 EXPLORER GUIDE

TIDES

AN EXPLORER'S GUIDE TO TIDES

WILLIAM THOMSON

3 EXPLORER GUIDE

THE MOON

AN EXPLORER'S GUIDE TO THE MOON

WILLIAM THOMSON

www.imray.com